Ferrari

FERRARI

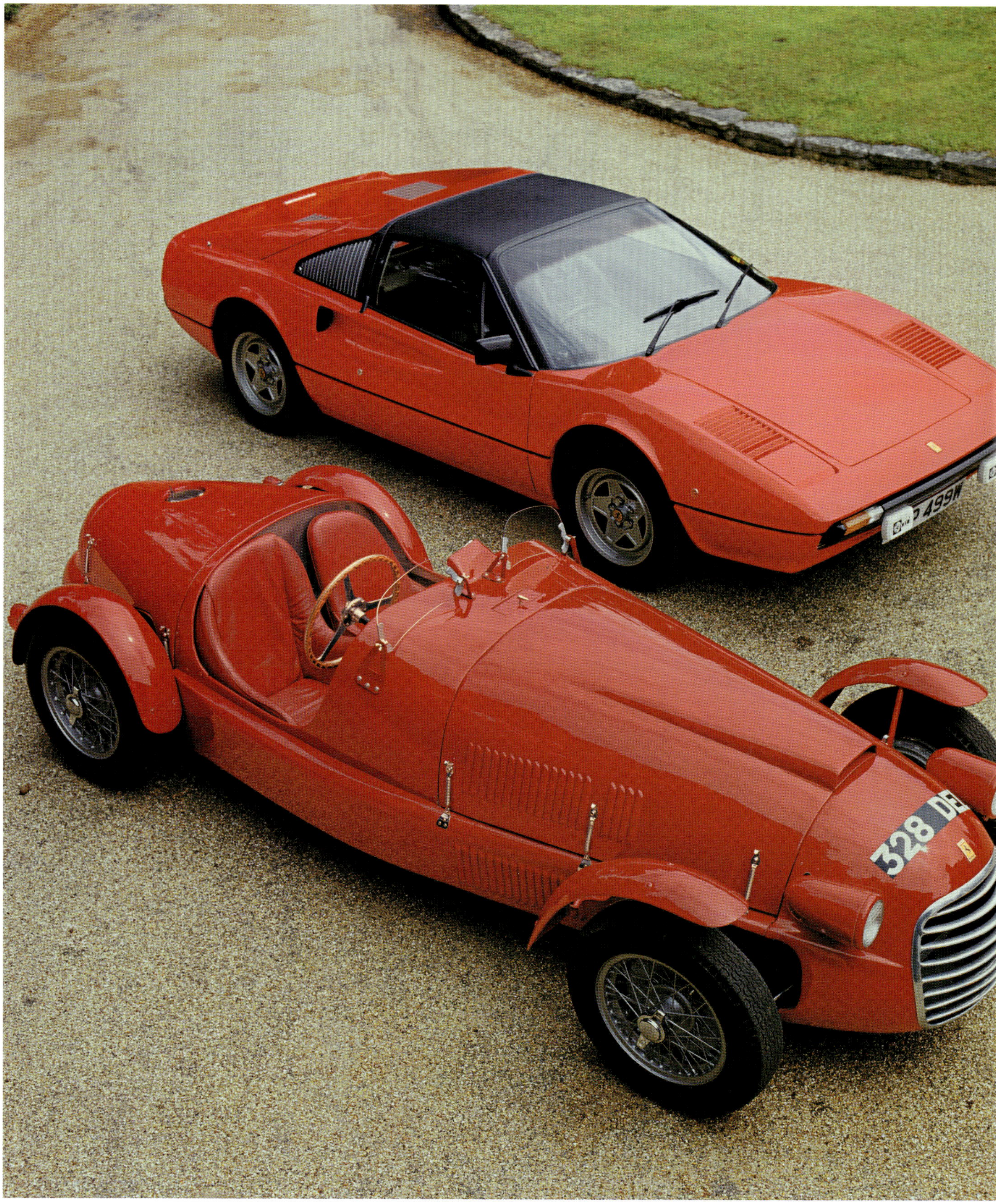
328 DE

MARKS & SPENCER

FERRARI

Andrew Charman

Marks and Spencer plc
PO Box 3339
Chester CH99 9QS
T21/8285/0412 C.I.F.A-37002516
www.marksandspencer.com

A copy of the CIP data for this book is available from the British Library upon request.

Created, designed, produced and packaged by Stonecastle Graphics Ltd

Designed by Paul Turner and Sue Pressley
Edited by Philip de Ste. Croix

Photographs © LAT Photographic Digital Archive
Photograph on page 1 courtesy of Ferrari UK
Printed and bound in Dubai

ISBN: 1-84461-304-6

Page 1: The Ferrari legend continues with the very latest Superamerica, a limited edition convertible based on the 575M Maranello, which goes on sale in 2005.

Page 2: More than a quarter of a century apart but equally desirable – the 166 Spider and 308 demonstrate the enduring appeal of Ferrari.

Page 3: Ferrari in the 1980s – the wedge noses that defined a generation of supercars.

CONTENTS

At the end of the 1950s Ferrari was still creating its cars primarily for competition, but the 250GT SWB (above) was also one of the most eminently suited to the road. Launched in 1959 the Compezione versions notched up a series of race wins and the more luxuriant Lusso proved a formidable road tourer. The car's 3-litre powerplant put out around 240bhp in road form.

IN THE CAR BUSINESS

Ferrari made its debut as a car manufacturer at the 1948 Turin Motor Show with two examples of its new 166, an Intercoupé (above right) and a Barchetta (above left), the latter name describing an open cockpit. Both were bodied by the Touring styling house – Ferrari only produced the rolling chassis. Over the first decade of the firm's existence its products were clothed by most of the great Italian coachbuilders.

THE FIRST FERRARI

Ferrari was finally able to build a car under his own name in 1947. It was called the 125, and was powered by an engine of 1500cc but V12 configuration, Enzo Ferrari always being a strong advocate of the 12-cylinder layout. Most 125s were upgraded to the specification of later models, the line effectively disappearing. This is the factory-built replica of the car.

INTRODUCTION

February 1898 – in the Italian town of Modena, Alfredo Ferrari and his wife Adalgisa celebrate the arrival of their second son, whom they name Enzo. Alfredo is a metalworker, and perhaps dreams of a similar engineering career for his son. Little does he know that one day Enzo will earn his home town global fame as the place where the most revered sports cars of all come from.

In fact the young Enzo briefly harboured ambitions of becoming a journalist, until aged 10 he went with his father to watch the Coppa Florio road race. From that moment he knew he would be a racing driver. He competed throughout the 1920s in such high profile events as the Targa Florio, but, dogged by ill-health, he enjoyed little success. When his own son Dino was born in 1932, Ferrari moved into a role that he was better suited for, as a race team manager.

Ferrari had been working for Alfa Romeo, which allowed him to form his own race team, and throughout the 1930s Scuderia Ferrari was effectively the official Alfa works squad. It proved very successful until German giants Mercedes-Benz and Auto Union invaded the Grand Prix scene. Shortly before the Second World War Ferrari went back to working for Alfa Romeo, but he soon fell out with his fellow management and with a few colleagues left to set up on his own.

The leaving agreement with Alfa Romeo prevented Ferrari from using his own name on a car for four years, so he set up an engineering consultancy, Auto Avio Costruzione, entering two cars under this name in the 1940 Mille Miglia road race. Then war intervened, and by the time peace returned in 1945 Ferrari was free to build his own cars. The legend had begun...

The first car to wear Ferrari's famous prancing horse badge, the 125 of 1947, has not survived. This is a replica built by the Ferrari factory.

CHAPTER ONE

BUILDING THE LEGEND

Italy was shattered after the war but Enzo Ferrari was not one to refuse a challenge. From his factory in Maranello, just south of Modena, he boldly announced his intention to build Grand Prix and sports racing cars under his own name. The prototype Ferrari, the 125 of 1947, astounded onlookers as its engine was of only 1.5 litres but was a V12 – this configuration a Ferrari favourite. It led its first race and won its second. Its successor, the 166, won the 1949 Le Mans 24 Hours, and from it evolved the first of the road cars. Ferrari marketed these for one reason – to provide money for racing.

The early history of the road cars is highly complex. Ferrari made only the chassis and powerplant of each car sold – clothing them was entrusted to various renowned Italian coachbuilders, and no single stylist was favoured over the others. Many early Ferraris were bodied by Vignale, but other notable interpretations were created by Touring, Ghia and by the styling house that would soon become synonymous with the products of Maranello, Pinin Farina.

Ferrari constantly developed its products, particularly the engines, and it was rare for two cars of ostensibly the same type to be truly identical. To add further confusion, many Ferraris served a dual purpose. Cars bought for use on the road were raced at weekends, while pure racers were exercised on public roads. And if such an excursion ended in an unfortunate meeting with the scenery, the owner simply had a new body built, often different to the one the car had originally been supplied with.

By the mid-1950s the still very young Ferrari company had produced more models than many much older manufacturers. Enzo's cars were expensive, but continuing success on the race track was making ownership of a Ferrari highly desirable to a growing number of sports-minded motorists.

ENZO'S ANONYMOUS AUTO

Enzo Ferrari left Alfa Romeo in 1939 with a pay-off, but he had to agree not to compete under his own name for four years. Within a year he used Fiat models as the basis for two small sports cars, built at his newly-created Auto Avio Costruzione engineering consultancy. Both were entered in the 1940 Mille Miglia as 815s, because they had eight cylinder 1.5-litre engines. Both retired from the race, and then war work interrupted Ferrari's racing ambitions.

SOLE SURVIVOR?

The 166 (above) was merely a development of the 125 with a bigger 2-litre engine. An example of this Spyder Corsa version, with its open-wheel body and wheels shrouded by cycle-style mudguards, is thought to be the earliest surviving Ferrari. However at this time all the cars from Maranello were built primarily for racing, and were constantly modified and renumbered, so its provenance cannot be completely proven.

BOROUGH NEWS
unshine
ast Daily
POOLS
Marlboro
SUPER
AMPOL
Sun
POLICE
TRICKED
JOH
INQUIRY
TOLD

BIGGER ENGINES FOR BETTER POWER

Within three years the engines in the 166 model line were enlarged to create the 195 (left) and 212 range. The model number of each car was derived from the cubic capacity of one cylinder – each in the 166's 2341cc engine measured up at 195.1cc, and 212cc in the 2.56-litre 212. The 340 America Berlinetta of 1951 (above) followed this practice, which Ferrari used on most of its early cars.

ANY STYLE YOU LIKE

At this time Ferrari's cars were still being bodied by a wide selection of coachbuilders, and even individual styling houses made changes between cars. This 212 is the work of Vignale, one of the most prolific stylists of the time, which produced a wide variety of designs on Ferrari's chassis.

ROOFLESS EFFICIENCY

The 225 Sport (above and right) appeared in 1952, basically yet another engine variation, this time with a 2.7-litre unit. This open spider version boasts trademark Vignale styling cues with its vertical cooling grilles either side of the radiator and the 'portholes' in the body sides. The car was also offered as a closed coupé.

SISTERS IN STYLE

The arrival of the 250MM and 340MM models in 1952 marked the start of the gradual rationalization of the styling applied to Ferrari's cars, and a swing towards the designs of Pinin Farina (right), though Vignale was also favoured. It built three specially-bodied 340s for the 1952 Carrera Panamericana road race in South America, calling them Mexicos (above).

RACING CERTAINTY

This 250MM Pinin Farina Berlinetta has clear racing cues, especially the easy-access fuel filler atop the boot. The body was formed from aluminium while power came from a 3-litre V12 engine. A demonstration of how easy it is to confuse Ferrari's cars at this time is the fact that the 250 was developed from the visually almost identical 342, and itself grew into the 340 which had the same 4.1-litre V12 powerplant as was in the 342.

The 250 GTO, the car that brought Maranello so much race success and is still one of the most desirable Ferraris today.

CHAPTER TWO

STYLE BY PININFARINA

Ferrari hit a milestone in 1953 when annual production for the first time exceeded 50 cars. The firm had grown in the space of a few years from race car specialist to serious road car manufacturer, but such growth required a change in thinking. Despite the quality of the mechanical parts, Ferrari products were still primarily associated with whichever design house had provided the body. But now Ferrari needed its own identity, and to rationalize its model line.

The answer lay with Pinin Farina. The Turin-based stylist had first clothed a Ferrari in 1951, and its elegant designs had since found increasing favour with Enzo Ferrari. Pinin Farina was also highly experienced in production-line car manufacture, a depth of knowledge that Ferrari badly needed. From 1954 Ferrari road car production was placed almost entirely in the hands of Pinin Farina, and not until 1973 would another stylist be permitted to put its body on a mainstream car from Maranello. The effect of such product focusing was dramatic – by 1960 Ferrari was turning out more than 250 cars a year, a figure that would double within the course of a few more years.

The first serious model lines produced under the partnership between Ferrari and the soon subtly renamed Pininfarina were the 250 Europa and 375 America of 1953. These were visually similar but fitted with different-sized engines. Within a year the 250 was developed into the 250 Europa GT. It boasted a shorter wheelbase, made possible by a newly developed and more compact 3-litre V12 engine, and it set a precedent. The 250 series of cars would account for most of Ferrari's production over the next decade, particularly the coupé of 1958 and its cabriolet sister that followed in 1959.

Such success, however, resulted in other manufacturers looking enviously at the sports car maker from Maranello...

RACE-BRED ROAD TOURERS

Typical of the growing synergy between Ferrari chassis and Pininfarina bodies was the 375MM PF Berlinetta (right) of 1953. Its race lineage was obvious, with the headlights placed under plexiglass covers. At the same time Ferrari offered the 250 Europa (below), its first serious Grand Tourer for those who expected comfort alongside performance. All the 64 cars made were bodied by Pininfarina. They were seemingly very similar but the first 20 were powered by 3-litre Lampredi V12 engines, while the rest, dubbed 250 Europa GTs, used a Columbo-designed engine that sat in a wheelbase shortened by 8in (200mm).

375 DAL

SPEED AND STYLE STATESIDE

The Ferrari success story spread across the globe and consistent race-winning performances in America soon created a big demand Stateside for the road cars. Ferrari responded by creating exclusive, luxury models for this market, though they were also much admired and sought-after worldwide. The 410 Superamerica was based on the earlier 375 America and was powered by a 340bhp 4.9-litre V12, again the work of Alfredo Lampredi. Just 34 were made between 1956 and '59.

CALIFORNIA DREAMING

America not only proved a rapidly-growing market for Ferrari, it inspired new models. Dealers in California predicted big sales for a convertible, and in 1958 Ferrari answered their pleas with the 250GT California Spider (right). It was built in various versions, with no two being completely the same. Unusually for the period the bodywork was made by Scaglietti, the coachbuilder more closely associated with Ferrari's competition cars.

7 HLA

NINO
NINO
1474 W 21

A FERRARI FOR FOUR

Pininfarina came up with a new design in 1958, updating the 250GT into the GT C, or coupé. It had a more delicate look than its predecessor, and was offered in both closed and open cabriolet versions, the latter (left) boasting a folding metal roof. Meanwhile the Maranello factory was working on its first production 2+2, which appeared in 1960 as the 250 GTE (above). It proved a big hit, almost 1000 eventually being made, and greatly boosted Ferrari's finances.

AN ICON FROM ITALY

To many the 250GTO (below) is the epitome of everything that is special about Ferrari. On the track this car beat all-comers, on the road it was the most desirable of transport. Today you could pay £5 million for one. Just 34 examples were built over two years, the majority for racing. It was developed from the 250 GT SWB, and curiously its shell, while so distinctive a shape and instantly recognizable as a Ferrari, was created not by Pininfarina but by Ferrari employee Giotto Bizzarrini. Meanwhile those who needed something a little less all-out racer, but not quite a pure luxury road car, could from 1962 buy the attractive 250GT Berlinetta Lusso (right).

1964 KO

TCH 100

EXPENSIVE BUT EXCLUSIVE

The 410 Superamerica was a luxury Ferrari, but the 500 Superfast of 1964 (left) took matters a stage further. Just 36 examples of this 2+2 were built, power again coming from a 5-litre V12, by now offering a whopping 400bhp. Everything about this enormous car dripped exclusivity, from the Pininfarina shell to the plush leather interior. Indeed it was very expensive to buy – but then many did dub it 'the best car in the world'.

UNDERRATED EXCELLENCE

Ferraris were traditionally quite demanding cars to drive and to live with, and paradoxically any model that did not live up to this reputation was regarded with less reverence than other models – often unfairly. The 330 GT of 1964 (above) was just such a beast. Like its predecessor the 250GTE, it offered space for four, at a pinch, but despite its 4-litre V12 engine the car was less overtly sporting and more comfortable to travel in. It was also the first production Ferrari to wear twin headlights.

SMOOTH OPERATOR

In the mid-1960s Ferrari road cars faced plenty of competition from the likes of Jaguar with the E-Type and the Miura of fellow Italian maker Lamborghini. Maranello's answer was the 275GTB (above), its beautiful Pininfarina body boasting bulging rear wings and headlights smoothed out under plexiglass covers. There soon followed an open-top GTS version (right) but its shell bore little relation to its Berlinetta sister's, while the engine, V12 of course, offered only 260bhp instead of the GTB's 280.

The gorgeous, twin-turbocharged and phenomenally fast 288GTO of 1984, capable of 0–62mph (100km/h) in under five seconds, very quickly earned itself supercar status.

CHAPTER THREE

NO LONGER INDEPENDENT

Ferrari's growth brought attention from major car manufacturers, but it was the sporting success of the cars from Maranello that led to the first serious takeover attempt. During the early 1960s American giant Ford made a serious bid to buy Ferrari, desiring the sporting reputation that went with the prancing horse badge. But on the brink of a deal Enzo pulled out, a decision that would soon lead him into the arms of another manufacturer rather closer to home.

Incensed, Ford management was determined to beat Ferrari on the race track, particularly at Le Mans, and soon they did so with the GT40 programme, immediately followed by the creation of the legendary Ford DFV Grand Prix engine. Ferrari was forced to pour funds into the racing business just to stay competitive with its American rival. This could not go on for long, so Ferrari turned to Italy's biggest car manufacturer Fiat – the two were already co-operating on an engine for use in Formula 2 racers and a new Ferrari road car. This was named the Dino in memory of Enzo's son, lost to illness aged only 24, and some Fiats also carried Dino badges. In 1969 Fiat agreed to buy half of the Ferrari road car business, this share to increase to 90 per cent on Enzo's death. He would remain in sole charge of the race team.

Life at Maranello continued much as before, though Fiat's influence at board level encouraged further growth. In 1971 Ferrari broke the thousand-cars-a-year milestone, making 1246. Most notable among them was the 365GT4/BB, a mid-engined model with the increasingly popular wedge-shaped body style. It debuted at that year's Turin Motor Show as an answer to growing competition from fellow Italian sports car maker Lamborghini, and it mapped out the future direction of Ferrari's road cars.

A FATHER'S TRIBUTE

When Enzo Ferrari decided to make a car as a tribute to his lost son Dino, it had to be special, and the Dino 206 GT of 1969 (above) was very different to what had gone before. Its 2-litre V6 engine offered 180bhp, tiny by Ferrari standards, but it was a type advocated by Dino himself. For the first time it was mid-mounted, between the wheels, in a lightweight aluminium shell. The Dino passed 62mph (100km/h) in under seven seconds and went on to 140mph (225km/h). Curiously the car and its 2.4-litre 246 successor carried no Ferrari badging, and were originally meant to be a marque of their own.

DAYTONA DAZE

Officially this car was the 365 GTB/4 (above), and merely an updated version of the previous 275GTB/4. But Ferrari fans quickly dubbed it the Daytona after Maranello's cars filled all three podium places at the 1967 Daytona 24-hour race. The Daytona came to be recognized as the greatest GT car on the market, and at 175mph (282km/h) the fastest, thanks to a V12 engine enlarged from 3.3 to 4.4 litres. Of course not everyone wanted such power and Ferrari filled the gap between cars such as the Daytona and its large luxury four-seaters with the 330 and 365 series, models such as the 365 GTC/4 (right) combining performance with comfort.

HPL 22K

KPD 634P

MOVING INTO MIDDLE AGE

The mid-engined Dino had proved a success and rivals Lamborghini and Maserati were moving towards similar layouts. Ferrari expanded on the theme with the 365GT4/BB (below), launched at the 1971 Turin show and intended to replace the Daytona, though initially the two were built alongside one another. The BB stood for Berlinetta, its body shape, and Boxer, its flat-12 engine. The same period saw the arrival of the 365 GT4 2+2 (left), Ferrari's most lavish four-seater yet. Evolving into the 400 series, they were for many years the most expensive Ferraris on the market.

RESISTING THE GERMAN RIVAL

Ferrari's big rival in the smaller sports car market was Porsche's four-seater 911, so the 308GT4 (above) was targeted directly at the German car. It was a mid-engined 2+2 with a trendy wedge nose, the first production V8-powered Ferrari, and – compared to some Maranello products – reasonably affordable. But it was crafted by Bertone, not Pininfarina, and considered too plain by many Ferrari enthusiasts. Early examples were named Dinos though it was never intended to replace the 246.

AUTOMATIC FOR THE PEOPLE

Automatic gearboxes – in Ferraris? Traditionalists were appalled but the demand was there, especially for the larger cars selling in the very important American market, and in the mid-1970s Ferrari bowed to pressure by offering auto as standard in its new 400 series (right). Successor to the 365 GT4 2+2, these were the most luxurious of Ferrari 2+2s, and powerful too, with 4.8-litre V12 engines producing well over 300bhp.

C390 PPB

TPB 640S

SHAPE OF THINGS TO COME

The 365GT4/BB proved that mid-engined larger cars were acceptable to buyers and in 1976 it evolved into the 512BB (left), so named because it had a 5-litre 12-cylinder engine. It established a familiar look for a decade, with its deep spoiler and brake cooling ducts along the flanks. The 512 and its fuel-injected successor the 512i were produced until 1984, then making way for the radical Testarossa.

HIGH IN FIBRE

When Ferrari eventually replaced its much-loved Dino, the successor had to be a clear relation, yet equally different to the norm. The 308GTB of 1976 (above) fulfilled the brief on all counts. It was built for almost a decade during which it became Ferrari's most popular model. The mid-mounted 3-litre V8 offered 255bhp, while the shell was designed in glassfibre by Pininfarina, back in favour after mediocre reviews for Bertone's 308GT4. Later versions switched to steel bodies, and in 1985 a revised 328 model extended the success story by another five years.

BACK TO FAMILIAR GROUND

Maranello's first Porsche 911 competitor, the 308GT4, had foundered on Bertone's bodywork. Pininfarina penned its successor, the Mondial 8 of 1980, and this four-seater (left) proved rather more of a hit, its 13-year production run spawning four versions and both coupé and convertible body styles. It was not the fastest Ferrari however. Initially powered by a 3-litre V8, it was the first production Ferrari with fuel injection as standard, but it offered only 214bhp. Meanwhile sales of the 308/328 range were kept buoyant by the launch of a targa-roofed model, the GTS (above).

THE FIRST SUPERCAR?

Today enthusiasts argue over which is the most desirable Ferrari of all, but the 288GTO (above) is certainly a contender. Like the 250GTO of two decades earlier, it was aimed at dominating racing, but the 288 never had a chance to prove itself as the category it was made for was scrapped before a race was run. So Ferrari built 272 as the most special of road cars. They might have looked a lot like a muscled-up version of sister machine the 308 but under the shell were exotic materials and a 2.9-litre twin-turbo V8 with 400bhp on offer.

The brand new F430 has been officially dubbed as the first of a new generation of Ferrari V8s. It emphatically proves that its builders have not lost the touch that first made ownership of a Ferrari so desirable more than half a century ago.

CHAPTER FOUR

MODERN TIMES

The BB in Ferrari's 365GT4/BB model name stood for Berlinetta Boxer, marking a change from V12 to flat-12 engines. The first examples were delivered to customers in 1973 just in time to weather the worldwide oil crisis that briefly made big-engined cars unpopular. The 365's mid-engined layout became the norm for the majority of the road car models that followed, including smaller V8 models. These included the Dino 308GT4 of 1973, penned not by Pininfarina but by rival Bertone. While a very neat car, it was initially thought somewhat bland, and when the 308GT4 was replaced by the Mondial 8 in 1980 Pininfarina again took charge of the looks.

The V8/mid-engine coupé theme continued in the 348 series, and then the 355 series, while there were also special editions – the twin-turbo 288GTO of 1984, and the F40 of 1987. Built to celebrate 40 years of production, this machine with its big faired-in rear wing became an instant pin-up for thousands of small boys. Its legacy would be continued in the V12-engined F50 of 1995, and today's most desirable Ferrari, the F60 Enzo, launched in 2002 and quickly sold out.

Not all Ferraris were mid-engined. The 400 series of the 1970s retained the classic front-engined rear-wheel-drive layout, and while throughout the 1980s range-topping Ferraris, such as the 200mph (322km/h) Testarossa, boasted a mid-mounted engine, advances in suspension technology saw a return to the traditional layout with the 1993 456GT and the 550 Maranello series of 1998.

Enzo Ferrari died in 1988, months after celebrating his 90th birthday. But while the man was gone, his legacy remained. Fiat's stewardship has seen continued expansion, including the takeover of fellow manufacturer Maserati in 1997, and today Ferrari flourishes both on road and track. Ownership of a car bearing the prancing horse badge remains a dream for many, experienced by a lucky few.

E272 DPK

STRAKES ALIVE

When the 512BB reached the end of its life in 1984, few were prepared for what replaced it. The Testarossa (left and below) was not only extremely wide, it was incredibly distinctive, its body boasting deep strakes running down either side into the radiator intakes. The 5-litre flat-12 engine was mid-mounted, but offered 390bhp, 50 horses more than the 512, making the Testarossa capable of a 5.2-second 0–62mph (100km/h) time and a 180mph (290km/h) top speed. More than 5600 Testarossas were made over seven years before it was updated to become the 512TR/M range.

THE ULTIMATE ROAD RACER

The F40 (above and top) was the modern interpretation of Ferrari's original ethos – racing cars that were usable on the road. Created from a stillborn race project and clothed in one of the most attractive bodies Pininfarina had created, its 475bhp twin turbo V8 produced a 0–62mph (100km/h) time of 4.2 seconds and a 201mph (323km/h) top speed. Fittingly, the F40 was the last road model unveiled by Enzo Ferrari himself in July 1987, 14 months before he died.

LONG WAY TO THE TOP

The 348 (below) was made for only five years from 1989, but it became one of Maranello's biggest sales successes, selling more than 9000 copies. Its mid-mounted 3.4-litre V8 engine remained mid-mounted, as in its predecessor the 328, but it was rotated to lie longitudinally in a chassis of pressed rather than tubular steel. With a top speed of 165mph (266km/h) and a 5.5-second 0–62mph (100km/h) time the 348 wore the prancing horse badge as proudly as its bigger-engined sisters.

PAST PRESENT

In sculpting the beautiful 456 of 1992 (above), Pininfarina had clearly derived much inspiration from the short-lived 365GT/C of two decades earlier. But while retro-looking, this front-engined 2+2 was a very modern Ferrari, its 442bhp 5.5-litre V12 endowing the car with performance comparable with its more overtly sporting two-seater sisters. Little wonder that more than a decade later it was still being made.

POWER SHIFT

The 355 (right), launched in 1994, was the fifth generation of a series that had begun with the 308 of 1975. The chassis was much changed while the 3.5-litre V8 engine boasted a 40-valve head, its 380bhp the most of any road Ferrari V8. Ferrari offered the car in Berlinetta, Targa and Spider variants.

EHF 1

36
S° DALMAZIO

GEARING UP, FORMULA 1-STYLE

The F355 may have been very different from its immediate predecessor the F348, but the big headlines surrounded its transmission. Ferrari fitted the car with the first road version of the semi-automatic gearbox used on the Formula 1 racers. Complete with steering-wheel shift paddles, it was vastly superior to any rival and overshadowed the performance of the rest of the car.

BACK TO THE FRONT

By the mid-1990s, Ferrari felt able to return to tradition even with its two-seaters. The 550 Maranello (left), replacement for the 512 line, returned to a front-engine rear-wheel-drive format. As a result the cabin was quieter and offered more room, while advances in suspension technology cut the previous handling advantages of mid-engined cars. Power was supplied by a 485bhp 5.5-litre V12, giving a 0–62mph (100km/h) time of 4.3 seconds and a 199mph (320km/h) top speed.

VERY SPECIAL BIRTHDAY GIFT

In 1995 Ferrari marked half a century of existence, and the celebration centrepiece was rather special. The limited edition F50 (above) drew heavily on the technology used by the F1 team. Its body and chassis were moulded in Kevlar and carbon fibre composites, and within was mounted a 4.7-litre V12 engine offering 520bhp and developed directly from the 1990 GP car's powerplant. The F50 could reach 62mph (100km/h) from rest in 3.7 seconds and power on to 202mph (325km/h), and it was versatile too – when the sun came out the hardtop could be removed. Just 349 were built between 1995 and '97.

RACING CERTAINTY

By 1999 the 355 was still selling well but Ferrari management felt it was time for an update. The resultant 360 (below) was an all-new car with Pininfarina again creating a look completely different from any predecessor. The frame was built largely of aluminium, 30 per cent lighter but almost 40 per cent stiffer than the 355's. The V8 engine was redesigned to offer 400bhp, 20 more than the F355. A successful one-make race series added to the 360's credentials, leading to the creation of a stripped-out homologation special version, the Challenge Stradale.

THE BOSS WOULD HAVE BEEN PROUD

How do you improve on a supercar such as the F50? Ferrari did just that in 2002 with the phenomenal F60 (left and above), the fastest road car to come out of Maranello. Its 6-litre V12 engine offered 650bhp and a top speed of 217mph (349km/h). The shell was pure Formula 1, even to the raised nose. Just 349 were built and sold only to customers pre-approved by Ferrari. But by far the greatest tribute to the F60 is that it was deemed worthy of being given the most evocative Ferrari name of all – Enzo.

SPACE – THE FINAL FRONTIER?

The latest four-seater from Ferrari, launched in 2004 to replace the 456M, is an all-aluminium wonder and another departure from previous practice – the 612 (above) boasts interior space far roomier than a typical 2+2. Power is supplied by a 5748cc V12 engine offering 540bhp, almost 100 horses more than the 456M, while the car takes the name of Scaglietti, a coachbuilder who worked closely with Ferrari in the earliest days and who was an expert in the crafting of aluminium.

THE LEGEND CONTINUES

The next chapter of the story. The F430 (following pages) was revealed in 2004, a car almost entirely created from the knowledge gained by Ferrari's all-conquering Grand Prix team. Its lightweight 4.3-litre V8 engine offers 490bhp, while the car bristles with technology. Highlights are the first electronic differential on a road Ferrari and a rotary switch on the steering wheel enabling the driver to control the car's various systems, just as Michael Schumacher does on his F1 car. The F430 is clear evidence that Enzo's legacy is safe in a new millennium.

The racing history of the Ferrari F1 team is long and glorious, but in recent years Michael Schumacher has become its greatest champion. 2004 brought his seventh World Championship, five of them in Ferraris.

CHAPTER FIVE

PRANCING HORSEPOWER

Enzo Ferrari often said that he only produced road cars to pay his racing bills, and the Ferrari badge is synonymous with competition – the only team to compete continuously in the Formula 1 World Championship from its inception in 1950 to the present day. In the 1950s, cars with the prancing horse on their flanks dominated the Grand Prix scene, and today Michael Schumacher is rewriting all the record books at the wheel of a Ferrari.

Enzo Ferrari started his career running Alfa Romeo's racing team and, when his own cars entered Grand Prix racing, it was the Alfas they had to beat. It did not take long – a record begun by Alberto Ascari, champion in 1952 and '53, has produced 182 race wins, 14 Drivers' World Championships and 14 constructors' titles to the end of 2004. And the success was not restricted to the Grand Prix scene – Ferrari dominated sports car events, clocking up nine Le Mans 24 Hour wins, and also victories in the great 1950s road races, the Mille Miglia and Targa Florio.

Tragedy has always accompanied success, however. Ascari was killed in a Ferrari race car in 1955, days after escaping when his F1 car plunged into Monaco harbour. Other fatalities included German Wolfgang Von Trips, who died with 16 spectators at Monza in 1961, and Gilles Villeneuve, regarded by many as one of the greatest ever F1 drivers, killed in a fearsome accident at Zolder in 1982. Personal tragedy has had its effect too – after his son Dino's death from illness in 1956, Enzo Ferrari never attended another race meeting.

As this book is written, Ferrari controls Formula 1 like never before, having won six straight constructors' titles and brought Michael Schumacher five of his seven world championships. The red prancing horses of Maranello are again the cars to beat.

FROM THE START

When the Formula 1 World Championship for Drivers began in 1950 there were Ferraris on the grid, but the Alfa Romeo team that Enzo Ferrari had formerly headed was dominant. The cars from Maranello would not take their first victory until midway through the 1951 season, Argentinian Froilan Gonzalez (above) triumphing at Silverstone in the Ferrari 375. When team-mate Alberto Ascari followed up with wins in Germany and at his home Italian GP, Alfa realized it could not match its young upstart rival, and quit Formula 1.

NO FORMULA TO FOIL FERRARI

With Alfa gone, Formula 1 organizers, the FIA, feared a Ferrari walkover so new rules for 1952 were based around less powerful Formula 2 engines. Ferrari responded with the four-cylinder 170bhp Tipo 500, and with rival Juan Manuel Fangio sidelined by an accident Ascari (left) won every Grand Prix he started, four Ferraris topping the championship. It was a similar story the following year, but the wins were shared around, five to Ascari and one each to team-mates Giuseppe Farina and rising English star Mike Hawthorn. But a return to big engines and the big budget of Mercedes would knock Ferrari off the podium for two years.

LONG ROAD TO SUCCESS

While dominating Formula 1, Ferrari remained unbeatable in the arena where Enzo had enjoyed his earliest triumphs, the long road races, particularly the Mille Miglia, a 1000-mile (1609km) endurance event around the roads of Italy. Between 1948 and the demise of the race in 1957, only twice were the Maranello cars beaten. Ferrari also won the first World Sports Car Championship in 1953, but regular success at Le Mans (above) proved more difficult. Having won the race in 1949 Ferrari did not repeat the feat until 1954, Maurice Trintignant and Froilan Gonzalez triumphing in the 375MM. But Ferrari's golden sports car years were just beginning.

RACING SUCCESS

Ferrari now entered its golden age of sports car racing. A second World Sports Car Championship title followed in 1954, three in a row in 1956-58, and wins again in 1960 and '61. But Le Mans proved elusive, and not until a very wet race in 1958 did the French 24-hour race trophy again go to Maranello, Phil Hill and Olivier Gendebien driving the 3-litre V12-engined 250 TR through the rain to victory (above). Aston Martin won the following year, but soon the sports car trophy cabinet at Maranello would need seriously enlarging.

TRIUMPH AND TRAGEDY

The 1957 season was the first in which Ferrari failed to win a Grand Prix, its Lancia-based cars no match for another Italian rival, Maserati. So – new for 1958 – was the Dino 246, named after Enzo's son who had died in 1956, while Maserati quit following losses sustained by a disastrous effort to beat Ferrari in sports car racing. Mike Hawthorn (right) won the championship by one point from Stirling Moss, cheering the Ferrari team following the death of Peter Collins in the German Grand Prix. Hawthorn then announced his retirement from racing, only to be killed in a road accident in January 1959.

GENEROUS TO A FAULT

Mercedes quit motor sport after the Le Mans disaster of 1955 that killed 80 spectators, while new Formula 1 competition from Lancia evaporated when the rival Italian maker ran out of money. The Italian government handed Lancia's cars to Ferrari for 1956 and driving the 'Lancia-Ferrari' Juan-Manuel Fangio won the championship, but only after unprecedented generosity from team-mate Peter Collins (above). In the final race of the season Collins handed his car, and his chance of becoming Britain's first World Champion, to Fangio after the Argentinian's developed steering trouble. Collins never became World Champion, and was killed in a Ferrari two years later.

THE SHARK BITES

Revolution hit Grand Prix racing in 1959 with the arrival of the rear-engined Cooper-Climax. Overnight its front-engined rivals, including Ferraris, were rendered obsolete. Maranello's response was slow, its first rear-engined car only built in time for the 1961 season and new regulations again based around Formula 2 with 1.5-litre engines. Many regarded the Tipo 156 (above), dubbed the 'shark-nose' due to its distinctive front end, as the most beautiful F1 Ferrari yet. Team-mates Phil Hill and Wolfgang Von Trips dominated that season, the American winning the title. Unfortunately the German perished with 16 spectators in an accident during the Italian GP at Monza.

ENDURING SUCCESS

Now Ferrari was back on top in Grand Prix racing, and no-one could come close to the cars from Maranello in sports cars either. Catalyst for this success was the beautiful GTO (above), a lowline Grand Tourer powered by a 280bhp 3-litre V12 engine and soon to become a Ferrari legend. It established itself as the unbeatable combination once the FIA declared that the World Championship for Sports Cars would be run to road car-based GT regulations from 1962. Ferrari took a hat-trick of titles between 1962 and '64, and was equally dominant in the Le Mans 24 Hours.

MID-LIFE CRISIS

Eventually the mid-engined revolution invading Grand Prix racing spread to sports cars, and Ferrari was ready. The 250P was based on the Dino 246 road car and built specially for Le Mans, winning in 1963 and '64. Its sister, the 250LM pictured here (left), was claimed to be merely a mid-engined variant of the GTO and thus acceptable under GT regulations, but Ferrari lost that argument. It still won at Le Mans in 1965 and rival Ford, envious of such success, responded by trying to buy Ferrari. When that bid failed, Ford built its own car, the legendary GT40, signalling the end of Ferrari's sports car domination.

FROM TWO WHEELS TO FOUR

From the mid 1960s Ferrari faced new Grand Prix challenges from the UK: Lotus and rising star Jim Clark, and Graham Hill at BRM. But the title returned to Maranello in 1964 – former motorcyclist John Surtees (above and right) became the first World Champion on two wheels and four, winning by a single point at the final race when championship leader Hill spun and Clark's engine seized. Surtees drove the Tipo 158, Maranello's first semi-monocoque car that used the engine as a stressed member with no separate chassis. Ferrari was now chasing technology created by the technically superior UK teams, and would not win another drivers' title for 11 years.

CLOSE BUT NO CIGAR

The balance of power in Grand Prix racing continued to shift away from the major manufacturers to the smaller specialist UK squads. Ford's superb DFV engine used by Lotus (and soon most of the grid) added to Ferrari's woes, and led to a brief withdrawal in 1969. But the team returned for 1970 with a new car, the 312B, and a new star in Belgian Jackie Ickx (above). In Austria Ickx and team-mate Clay Regazzoni lapped the entire field on their way to a dominant win, and the red cars triumphed three more times that year, but too late to snatch the World Championship.

THE CARS TO BEAT

For the 1974 Grand Prix season Ferrari signed a seemingly over-impetuous Austrian from BRM. By the middle of 1974 Niki Lauda (left) was a championship contender, and in the following season at the wheel of the superb 312T Lauda proved the class of the field to take the first of his three titles. This shot (below) was typical of the season, Lauda leaving reigning champion Emerson Fittipaldi in his wake. Lauda would probably have won a second title in 1976 but for a fiery accident at the Nürburgring. Weeks after being read the last rites and still severely burned, he returned to action, but too late to prevent James Hunt from taking the championship by a point. The following year, consistency in the T2 version of the 312 proved Lauda's secret weapon as faster rivals faltered. However, as the season went on, the Austrian's relationship with Ferrari soured, and having won the title with two races to spare he left the team. His replacement would become one of Formula 1's greatest heroes...

MICHELIN
Agip
12
HEUER
Agip
MICHELIN
Agip

A MAN CALLED GILLES

In a world where the stars were increasingly becoming business-orientated and frankly boring, French-Canadian Gilles Villeneuve was a racer in the old style. His car, here pictured at Montreal in 1978 (left), always appeared on the edge of control, an accident waiting to happen. Often there were accidents, and as a result when Ferrari claimed another drivers' title in 1979, it was not Villeneuve but Jody Scheckter (below) enjoying the plaudits. Gilles would no doubt have become World Champion, but then came 1982. From 1981 Villeneuve was paired with Frenchman Didier Pironi. Politics were now rife in Formula 1, and the 1982 San Marino GP was boycotted by most teams, leaving Ferrari with an easy run to victory. The two drivers played to the fans but agreed that Gilles would win, only for Pironi to pass him on the last lap. The pair went to the next race in Belgium not speaking, and minutes into a practice session Villeneuve died in a violent accident. Pironi's career was ended four races later by a crash that broke his legs.

WINNING CARS, FRUSTRATED DRIVERS

Despite the tragedies of 1982 Ferrari ended the year as top constructor, and won this title again the following year with the 126C3, campaigned with some success by René Arnoux (above) and Patrick Tambay but unable to match the consistent points scoring of Nelson Piquet at Brabham. Michele Alboreto would briefly feature in the 1985 title race, but not until 1990 would the red cars from Maranello be truly feared again.

IL LEONE AND THE PROFESSOR

Ferrari signed Nigel Mansell (above) for 1989 and when the Englishman won his first race for the team, fanatical Italian fans dubbed him 'Il Leone' – the lion. A year on he was joined by the most analytical driver of them all, 'Professor' Alain Prost (left), and the Frenchman duelled with his long-time rival, Ayrton Senna, for the championship. The battle went to Japan where the previous year the pair had collided, giving Prost the title. This time Senna simply drove Prost off the road to take the prize and rob Ferrari of its first drivers' championship in more than a decade.

CHAMPION OF CHAMPIONS

Michael Schumacher was already a champion when Ferrari signed the German in 1996, but his arrival in Maranello, along with team manager Jean Todt, team director Ross Brawn and designer Rory Byrne were the building blocks leading to today's domination, the likes of which had never been seen in Formula 1. Schumacher is pictured at Monaco (right) on his way to his first Ferrari title in 2000. He would probably have won it in 1999 had he not broken his leg at Silverstone, and he has taken four more since. Meanwhile Ferrari has won six straight constructors' titles – the legend of the cars from Maranello continues...

Marlboro
MAGNETI MARELLI
FedEx
BRIDGESTONE

INDEX